GRANDMA'S TREASURY

©Ward Lock Limited 1989

This edition published by Gallery Books,
an imprint of W.H.Smith Publishers Inc.,
112 Madison Avenue, New York, New York 10016

ISBN 0-8317-3953-3

Printed and bound in Czechoslovakia.

GRANDMA'S TREASURY

GALLERY BOOKS
An Imprint of W. H. Smith Publishers Inc.
112 Madison Avenue
New York City 10016

THE ARTIST

WEE Bobby always loved to draw ;
    He copied everything he saw ;
He drew the dog, he sketched the cat,
He shaded this, he painted that ;
And seeing that he was so small
His drawings were not bad at all.

His father, proud of what he drew,
Took him one morning to the Zoo.
Bob gazed on tigers, gaunt and grim ;
The kangaroos excited him ;
He viewed the tall giraffes with awe,
He'd never seen such necks before !

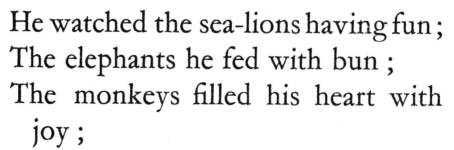

He watched the sea-lions having fun;
The elephants he fed with bun;
The monkeys filled his heart with
    joy;
He was a really happy boy.
        And when at last the day-
        light died,
        I must admit he almost
        cried!

        Next day, you should have
        seen the lad;
    He got out paper—all he had;
Then settled down re-
    solved to draw
The things he'd seen the
    day before.
But most of them, it
    must be said,
Had got well mixed
    within his head!

Two heavy horns he gave
the bear—
The sort you know they
never wear ;
The poor giraffe he made
so stout

He never could have
walked about !
The elephant was long
and thin—
'Twas quite a job to get
him in.

Ere long he'd used his
paper store,
So started drawing on
the door :

His Mother proud, per-
    ceiving it,
Began to worry just a bit.
" His   art,"   said   she,
  " keeps Bobby in ;
I think we'll teach him
  gardening."

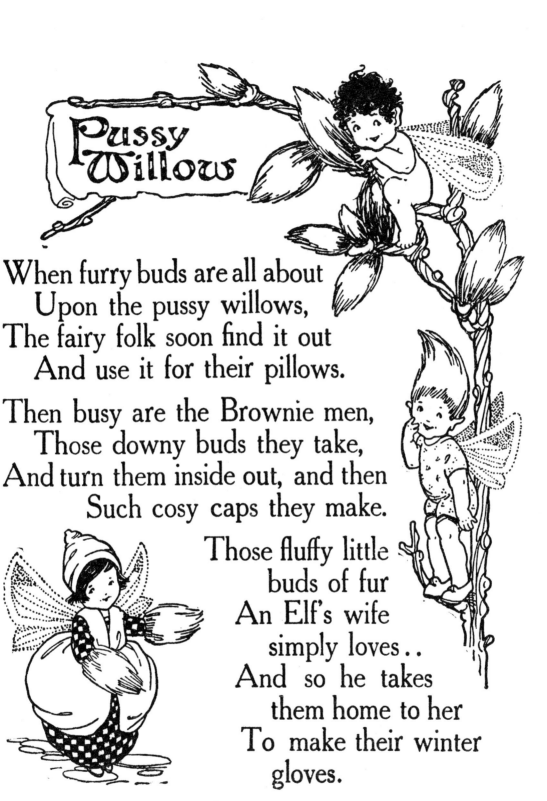

Pussy Willow

When furry buds are all about
   Upon the pussy willows,
The fairy folk soon find it out
   And use it for their pillows.

Then busy are the Brownie men,
   Those downy buds they take,
And turn them inside out, and then
   Such cosy caps they make.

Those fluffy little
   buds of fur
An Elf's wife
   simply loves..
And so he takes
   them home to her
To make their winter
   gloves.

9

My sister Molly and I fell out —
I'll tell you what it was all about.
She liked coffee and I liked tea,
And that was the reason we couldn't
agree !

THE SEA BABY

THE little Sea Baby was lost. She had gone for a ride on the back of a fish, and the fish had put her on the sea-shore to play for a while in a sand castle which some children had built. And while she was playing, a toy balloon had come along, and the Sea Baby had taken hold of the string. The balloon had sailed away up in the air with the Sea Baby holding on, until it had come down at last in the middle of a meadow miles away from the sea-shore.

The poor little Sea Baby was dreadfully frightened, for she didn't know in the least how she was to get back to the sea again. A dragonfly lent her a pair of wings, but the Sea Baby didn't know how to use them. She was almost in tears, when a little girl and a little boy came by.

The Sea Baby was frightened, but she plucked up courage and told them what had happened, and they fetched their big sister. Their big sister ran to tell an old woman who was half a fairy. The old woman lighted a candle and made a spell. And out of the candle came many fairies.

"Tell the fairies what you want," said the old woman. The sister told the fairies about the little lost Sea Baby. And they picked up the Sea Baby and flew with her back to the sea.

"THE SEA BABY WAS FRIGHTENED."

"A little fairy creature sprang out from the flame."

"One little imp pretended to drive Bobby as if he were a horse."

THE FAIRIES' RACE

"Fairies at last," shouted Bobby. He had always wanted to see fairies, but now he did see them. He knew they were fairies because they had wings. They teased him and laughed at him, and one little imp pretended to drive him as if he were a horse. But they were quite as nice as he had expected and Bobby never danced so well.

"Who's for the race?" they began to shout.

And very soon Bobby was watching the funniest race he had ever seen. One of the riders was on a chicken, another was pulled by a mouse, while another rode a snail, but the luckiest of the riders was carried by a big toad, who jumped over the last part of the course over the head of the mouse and won easily, whilst Bobby cheered like anything.

And just then when the prizes were being given out, he woke up, and heard the well-known voice of his nurse saying: "Time to get up and leave all the dreams behind."

"Bobby was watching the funniest race he had ever seen."

MY GARDEN

IF I'd a garden of my own,
   I'd grow all sorts of things,
Like pussycats and butterflies
   And birds with velvet wings.

Of toys, of course, I'd have a share,
   Tin soldiers, tops and beads ;
I shouldn't have to spend my time
   In pulling up the weeds.

TULIPS

Margaret W. Tarrant

SPRINGTIME IN THE GARDEN

PICTURE BOOKS

And lollipops and ginger-breads,
  And chocolates by the score :
So you could simply gather them
  If you should wish for more.

And picture books should blossom there,
  The finest that are grown :—
Perhaps it lies in Fairyland,
  That garden of my own.

PARTIES

IT'S fun, I know, on a winter's night
   To go to a party all in white,
But better by far, as you'll all agree,
Are the games we play by two and three;
The games we play, that nobody shares,
All by ourselves on the nursery stairs.

A party may play round a Christmas Tree
At "Little Puss, pretty Puss, come to me!"
"Hunt the slipper" or "Nuts in May,"

But better by far are the games we play,
With a knight and a dragon all our own,
And a princess nobody else has known.

A party is always so stiff and clean,
Starched and frilly : you know what I mean !
It's not like that in the games we play—
Any old smock in any old way
Will do for a queen or a Quaker friend
In the very best game of " Let's Pretend."

WHEN I WAS A LITTLE BOY.

When I was
a little boy
I lived by myself.
All the bread
and cheese I got
I put upon a shelf.
The rats and
the mice.
They led me
such a life,
I was forced to
go to London
To get myself
a wife.

My first is in mat, but not in rug;
My second's in dig, but not in dug;
My third is in vapour, & also in air,
My fourth is in lime, but not in pear.
My fifth is in rap, but not in knock,
My last is in mantle, but not in frock

My whole is the name of a girl.

CAN YOU DO THIS SIMPLE ACROSTIC?

SILLY DILLY

Old Reynard Fox
lived by himself
Just near a shady
wood
The Field Folk all avoided him
('Twas better that they should!

For if a rabbit or a hare
Or wild duck chanced to stray
Too near his den, they always seemed
To vanish on that day!)

Now by the pond beneath the hill
  Lived dear old Mother Duck,
She never went near Reynard, though
  She had a lot of pluck.

"It's much too risky, dears," she'd say,
  "And you must **never** go,
My little ducklings, near that wood,
  You might get caught, you know."

MOTHER DUCK

Now Dilly Duckling
was the last
Of Mother Duck's
big brood,
Conceited, too, she
was, and oft
More than a trifle
rude.

"I think you're much
too careful, then,"
She said, with beak
in air,
"So, Mother, if I
choose to go
Well, go I shall, so
there!"

And off she went, quite quite alone,
  The very selfsame day
Until she reached the wood. (Quite near,
  Old Reynard's homestead lay.)

The fox had seen her climb the hill
  And off he went to meet her,

                          And with a
                          bow and
                          flourish,
                          then
                          Did most
                          politely
                          greet her.

"A thousand welcomes, dear," he said, "Pray do come in, Miss Dilly, You must so need a rest. The way Up here is steep and hilly.

How nice you look! I've never seen
A duckling half so sweet.
Your feathers are so golden and
You have such dainty feet!

Come in and rest them, dearie, do.
You'd like some tea, no doubt!"

.   .   .   .   .   .

Poor silly Dilly went
    inside
His house . . .
But ne'er came
    out!

And next day when I chanced to meet
    Old Reynard in the heather,
Upon his coat I
    noticed more
Than one gay
    golden feather.

SKIPPING-TIME

"It's skipping-time," said Phyllis. How did she know that it was time to get out her skipping-rope? Nobody knows, but when the day came, she began to skip. Some little girls are very clever at this game. They can go on ever so long, and, when their friends are turning

"'It's skipping-time,' said Phyllis."

the rope, some can go on skipping, "salt, mustard, pepper!" and never seem to get tired. Others can dart in while the rope is turning and jump out again without once touching the rope.

There are some, too, who can do

tricks by crossing their hands, and can keep time with music.

Phyllis means to learn some new things this year before the time comes when she will put the rope away, for skipping-time does not last all the year. "I mean to skip with my hands crossed," she says; and it will be hard, but she will, for Phyllis is very determined and if she does not succeed the first time, she will try and try again until she does.

THE CANARY

Mary had a pretty bird
Feathers bright & yellow,
Slender legs – upon my word
He was a pretty fellow!
The sweetest notes he always sang,
Which much delighted Mary;
And near the cage she'd
ever sit,
To hear her own
canary!

THE SCOOTER

Now scooters are handy for us in the
day,

But they're handier by far in the
night,

When in dreams you get out with the
fairies to play,

With the moon and the stars for
your light.

Then your scooter will carry you down
the white clouds,

And faster and faster you run,

While the fairies with wings dance
around you in clouds,

Till the long steep journey is done.

(And there, just where it stood when
you went to sleep, is the old scooter.)

"While the fairies with wings dance around you in clouds."

THE BABY PUSSY

The black Pussy does not like anyone to touch her little kitten, that is to say, she does not like anyone but Annie, for Annie she counts as one of her own people. So she lets her take the baby in her arms for a walk.

" She lets Annie take the baby in her arms for a walk in the garden."

All pussies and dogs love Annie, and Pussy says to herself: "She will look after the little scamp, and give me a rest."

She feels so safe when Annie has her kitten, that Pussy will even let Annie take it out of sight, and will then venture out herself, but she's soon back again to see that "all's well" with Kitty.

THE ANIMALS MAKE FRIENDS

KITTY LITTER

THE SEARCH FOR FOOD

THE SAFEST PLACE

RICH
MRS. BOB-TAIL

At number two the Warren,
    Lived Mrs. Bob-tail Bun,
With all her little rabbits
    From Flap, the eldest son,
Right down to tiny Topsy,
    Who was the youngest one.

She'd scarcely any money,
    Her shoes were very worn,
Her aprons past all mending

Because they were so torn,
Yet Mrs. Bob-tail Bunny
Was not a bit forlorn.

"I always feel quite happy,"
Said Mrs. Bob-tail Bun
To Mrs. Leslie Long-ears,
Who lived at number one,
"We've **just** enough to keep us,
And life is full of fun!"

"My dear," said Mrs. Long-ears
    To Leslie, that same night,
"Poor Mrs. Bob-tail Bunny
    Is really not quite right!
She talks of being happy,
    Yet looks a perfect sight.

"She has that tribe of children!
    She's poor as she can be,
Her clothes are **so** old-fashioned,

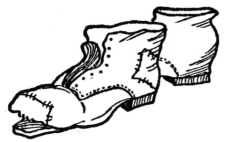

Her boots you ought
to see!
I'm glad I'm rich!"
But Long-ears
Said, "Listen, dear, to me,

"Though Mrs. Bob-tail Bunny
May scarcely have a cent
She's better off than we are,
I know just what
she meant.
She has what we
have **not,** my
dear,
—A great store
of Content!"

SOMETIMES, when I have had my tea and
when I have said my grace,
I run to meet my Daddy coming from the
office place ;
I run past all the houses, to the great big gate
that swings,
And then I have to stop because of motor-cars
and things.

I climb up on the gate and peep between the
top-most bars,
And watch the people passing and the horses
and the cars,
Until I see my Daddy, then I pull it open wide,
And he jumps off his bicycle and then I have
a ride.

PETER'S CAGE

WHEN Peter's shut up in his cage—
    A safe and cosy nook—
Mrs. and Master Teddy Bear
    Stroll up to have a look.
" My child," says Mrs. Teddy Bear,
" Look at that savage boy in there ! "

" Oh, will he eat me, Mummy dear ? "
   Says fluffy Master Ted.
" I do not know, I cannot tell,"
   His anxious Mummy said.
Then quacked the ducks, " If there's a doubt,
We're very glad he can't get out."

But Peter, stretching out his arm,
   Pulled all of them inside.
The ducks and Teddy Bears at first
   Were rather terrified.
But when they found the boy was tame
They all made friends and had a game.

45

"Bow-wow,"
says the
Dog.

"Mee-ow," says
the Cat.

"Grunt, grunt,"
says the Hog,

And "Squeak,"
says the
Rat.

"Tu-whoo", says
the Owl,

The Crow
says "Caw, caw,"

"Quack, quack,"
says the
Duck,

And the
Ass says
"Hee-haw!"

H.G.C.
Marsh
Lambert

The Story of A
CAKE

Clara cooked it
Auntie asked for it
Katie kept it
Enid enjoyed it.

THE PIXIE PIE

"Swing high, swing high,
Now I'm up in the sky,"

sang Pauline, as the swing took her up-up-up—almost to the top of the cherry-tree. Then down-down-down—she went again.

But as she was passing those upper branches she had seen something which made her grip the ropes of the swing tightly in her hands and fix her eyes on a branch above her head.

Up-up-up she went again, and as she passed that upper branch once more she raised herself in her seat and stared among the leaves and fruit.

Yes, there was no doubt about it!

Down went Pauline again, and this time she scraped her heels against the ground so that in another minute the swing had stopped. Then she got out, and scrambled quickly up into the branches of the old cherry-tree.

What had she seen?

Why, the first time she passed that upper branch, she felt sure that she had

 caught sight of a tiny wee man, dressed in a cook's apron and cap! And the second time she passed he was there still, only he had seen her, she was afraid, and if so, would he have disappeared when she reached the branch?

She scrambled on and up, and at last reached the branch. But the little man had gone! There was no trace of him anywhere.

Pauline felt so disappointed. "I'm **sure** he was a fairy cook," she said to herself. "Oh—whatever's that?"

She peeped in among the leaves as she spoke. There,

resting on a forked twig, stood a tiny pastry board and bowl, and next to them the sweetest little cherry pie you can possibly imagine!

"So the fairies love cherries as much as I do," said Pauline. "Poor little man, I expect he is dreadfully scared. I'll leave him in peace. But I wish he'd make a cherry pie for me!"

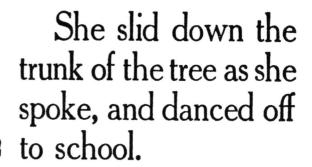

She slid down the trunk of the tree as she spoke, and danced off to school.

When she got home at dinner-time Pauline went out into the garden again and climbed to the top of the cherry-tree.

The pie was gone. So were the pastry things.

But when Pauline reached the ground again she found, on the seat of the swing, another tiny cherry pie! It was baked to a turn, and traced on the top of the crust, in funny, scrawly letters, she read "For Pauline, from the Pixie."

BY THE SEA

BY H.G.C. MARSH LAMBERT

I wandered on the reef and found
   A crimson jelly·fish.
I caught some prawns — enough to fill
   A little china dish.

I walked along the sandy shore,
   And caught a nice big crab
I went a·fishing from
      the pier,
   And caught a
     tiny dab.

I peeped into a pool and caught
   A star·fish, pink
     and gold.
   I fell into a bigger
      pool,
  And caught —
  — A horrid cold !

HOT WATER

BEST MUSTARD.

54

ON THE BEACH WITH BABY

HIGH, HIGH, HIGH IN THE SKY

"·WITH·THE·KITE·I·WISH·WE·COULD·FLY·
·THROUGH·THE·CLOUDS·AND·OVER·THE·SEAS·
·LOOKING·DOWN·ON·THE·MOUNTAINS·HIGH·
·AND·ON·BIRDS·AND·NESTS·IN·THE·TREES·"

HOW TEDDY HELPED

"My Daddy's such a busy man,"

Said Ted. "I'll help him all I can."

So off he went and hoed and raked

Until poor Teddy fairly ached.

Then over to the shed he ran

And fetched a great big watering can.

"I'll water all those lovely seeds,"
Said Teddy. (They
were only weeds).

And then he pruned
the roses too
Dear me, there was
a lot to do!—

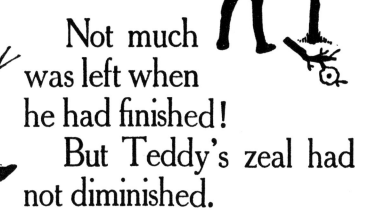

Not much
was left when
he had finished!
But Teddy's zeal had
not diminished.

Next for the poultry
yard he made
To gather up the
eggs, new-laid.

 But Rover jumped
against his
legs—

Down went poor Ted.
Down went the eggs.

"Dear me!" said Ted, "that is a waste.
There's more to do.   I must make haste

To find that tin of paint," he said,
"For Daddy means to paint the shed,

I'll do it for him."
(See him now
A smudge of
paint upon his
brow

With brush
and paint and
ladder, too
Oh yes, he
has a **lot** to
do.)

Now Ted is perched upon the shed
And painting it the brightest red,
When suddenly his father calls.
Poor Teddy jumps, then slips and falls
Right down upon the
ground below.

He's covered too from top to toe
With paint. "You'll go straight
off to bed

When you've been
washed," his Daddy
said.

(Ted's point of view he could not see.
'Twas rather hard. Don't you agree?)

LDMTHRHBBRDWNTTTHCPBRD,
 TGTHRPRDGGBN,
BTWHNSHGTTHRTHCPBRDWSBR,
 NDSTHPRDGGHDNN.

The vowels are all missing from this well-known rhyme.
Can you read it?

Turn to page 120 for the answer

My Cockatoo
     says
"How d'you do?"
— "Pretty Poll", and "Who are you?"
    She's lived with me
    Since I was three. —
My darling little Cockatoo!

H.G.C.
Marsh
Lambert

The New Babes in the Wood

TONY and Tess were going to a fancy dress party. Tess was going as Little Miss Muffet, and Tony as Little Tommy Tucker. When the day came at last, they were dressed long before it was time to start.

A taxi was coming to take them to the party, although the house wasn't far away, but their mother didn't want them to walk there in their fancy dresses. So, as soon as they were ready, Tony and Tess climbed on to a wooden chest below the drawing-room window and watched for the taxi.

" I wish it would be quick. Wouldn't it be dreadful if we were late for the party," said Tess.

Tony looked at the clock.

"We *are* late!" he cried. "The party is four o'clock and it's half-past four already."

"Oh dear! What shall we do?" said Tess, beginning to cry.

"We'll walk," said Tony. "We'll go by the short cut through the wood." And without even waiting to put on their hats and coats, Tony and Tess ran out of the house.

" 'WE'LL WALK,' SAID TONY."

But woods are difficult places to find your way in, and Tony and Tess lost themselves amongst the trees. They were dreadfully frightened, but luckily the gamekeeper came along and found them.

The game-keeper laughed when he heard about the party. "I guess your clock must be wrong," he said. "It's only just four now. Come along into my cottage and my wife will give you some milk and cakes while I

"TONY AND TESS LOST THEMSELVES AMONGST THE TREES."

go and tell your mother where you are. You say you are supposed to be Little Miss Muffet and Little Tommy Tucker? I should call you the Babes in the Wood."

He took Tess and Tony into his cottage, which was quite near, and then went and told their mother. And in the end they got to the party—though their mother said they really did not deserve to go, because they had been so naughty to run away.

"If you had come to me, I could have told you that the clock in the drawing-room had stopped," she said.

Tony and Tess were very late for the party and missed quite a lot of it. But I think that served them right.

"THE GAMEKEEPER'S WIFE BROUGHT THEM MILK AND CAKES."

IN SCHOOL

WHEN I'm sitting next to Fanny, oh, we're very, *very* good
For we do just simply ev'rything that Teacher says we should;
And we're always very punctual—oh, we're never, *never* late;
And we answer ev'ry question, and we sit up very straight;
But—I can't help thinking sometimes when I'm tired of being good,
That I'd like to sit by Bobby at the bottom— yes, I *would*!

When I'm sitting next to Bobby, oh, I *am* a
    naughty girl !
For I let him eat my lunch and pull my hair
    right out of curl ;
And we laugh and play a little, and I some-
    times pinch his hand,
And when Teacher asks a question, I don't
    seem to understand.
But when we're kept in after, then I cry my
    eyes away,
And wish I'd sat with Fanny and been very
    good all day.

"'We thought you would be hungry,' said the fairies."

THE LOVELY PICNIC

It is not very nice to have a picnic all alone, but there was no one to go with Janet. All the others were in School. So Janet went by herself into the fields and sat down, not very happy. But suddenly all round were fairies.

"We thought you would be hungry," said one, "so we've brought you some cakes."

"We thought you would like a dance," said another, "so up you get, and dance with us."

And presently the fairies became tired and all went to sleep under a big toadstool, so Janet quietly tip-toed away.

When Janet was home again, the other children said: "It must have been dull being all alone."

"But I wasn't alone," she answered.

"Presently the fairies became tired and all went to sleep under a big toadstool."

THE FAIRIES LOOKED AFTER HER

THE FAIRY LANTERN LIT THE SKY

THE PATHWAY OF LIGHT

"Who's for the Earth?"
　　Said the fairies bright,
Taking their place
　　On the pathway of light.

And the fairies come
　　From near and from far,
To ride to the Earth
　　On the light of the star.

And when they have danced
　　All the night, they go back,
By the way that they came
　　On the starry track.

THE QUACK

When she heard the loud "Quack!
Quack!"
She hid behind her brother's back;
For he was more than two years
older,
And more, much more, than two
years bolder.
So she hid and never stirred
While he faced the angry bird;
But still poor Jane, in spite of that,
Felt her heart go pitter-pat,
Till that very cheeky quack
On the children turned his back.

THE PRIZE DUCKS

That was the proudest day in the pond,
  When Mother Duck and her
                    children ten
Won the Prize at the Summer Show,
  And waddled home again;
  Each duck with a brother,
  They followed their mother
Two by two to the pond again.

"They took some of their Christmas presents and spread them where
Jack Frost would be sure to find them."

WHEN JACK FROST COMES

It was an old-fashioned Christmas,
and Jack Frost was coming every
night.

"What can we do for Jack
Frost?" the children asked. "Everybody has presents, but nobody ever
thinks of Jack Frost."

So one evening they took some of
their Christmas presents and spread
them where Jack Frost would be sure

to find them; and they put a card for
J. FROST, Esquire. When they came
the next day, they saw that he had
been there, because everything, the
chocolates and Christmas-tree and the

" The Snow Man seemed to join in the fun when they danced round."

other things were all so sparkling. Of course, when the snow was thick and crisp, they had to have an Old Snow Man. They made a big snow-ball for his body and a lesser one for his head; and Dad let them have an old hat and a pipe. He was the funniest old man, and seemed to join in the fun when they danced round.

"They made a big snowball for his body."

THE ELVES IN THE MOON

When the moon is round and white
On a clear and shining night,

Some can see an old man there
Looking at them with a stare.

Others see some dancing elves,
Just a little like themselves,

Dancing gaily in the light
When the moon is round and white.

THE UMBRELLA

When they went out for a walk, Mummy said: "Now, you must take an umbrella."

"Please, no!" they said. But Mummy was firm.

So they took the umbrella, saying: "What a pity we have to carry it."

But the skies began to grow black; and then a drop of rain fell, and another drop, and then hundreds. So they were very glad that Mummy had made them take the umbrella. When they came home, they shouted: "You were right, Mummy, and we are almost dry."

"Are you?" she said with a smile. "But I think you had better change your boots and stockings."

READY FOR THE PARTY

What a time it always takes
    Mummy, Nan and me
When they have to make me ready
    For an ordinary tea.

But when party days are come
    And I wear my party frock,
And the taxi comes
      at five,
They must start at
    three o'clock.

For Mummy works
    as well as Nan
To make me very
    spick and span.

POLLY AND PRUE

Polly and Prue were so cross,
  Fought for the sponge Dad had lent them;
Fido grew anxious and sad,
  Tried very hard to content them.

Polly cried: "Bad naughty Prue!"
  Prue shouted back: "I don't love you!"
Fido said: "Kiss, and be friends,
  Mistletoe's hanging above you!"

Quick both looked up—then they kissed—
  Let Fido scrub them and duck them,
Dry them and give them warm milk,
  And then into beddi-by tuck them.

THE TWO CATS

Said Pussy to the China Cat:
  "I don't think much of you!
Your neck is long and not too fat,
  Your face is ugly, too.
Your ribbon bow is poor and thin,
And all the while you sit and grin."

The China Cat replied: "My dear,
  I'm very much admired,
And one advantage, sitting here,
  Is, that I'm never tired.
My face is always bright and cheery,
I can't say that of yours, old dearie!"

LEARNING TO COOK

It's a very nice
thing when it's
tea-time to eat

A very big
slice of a very
rich cake.

It will be a much nicer and jollier treat

When a cake for yourself you can
make.

You must stand on a stool by the table;
and there

You find flour and sugar and spice,

You must learn from your mummy,
how long you must stir,
And how such a cake you can ice.

But Cook says it isn't so easy to make
As some people think, a be-autiful cake!

WHEN IT RAINS

When it rains on
    me and you
We have rooms
    to shelter in;
But what do little fairies do
When the storms begin?

I wonder if the mushrooms make
Umbrellas for the fairies wee,
And from the rain they shelter take,
Just like you and me.

And the raindrops patter, patter,
　　But beneath, with gauzy wings,
Fairy thinks it does not matter,
　　Sits her down and sings.

IN THE COUNTRY

It is lovely to wake up in the country. "Where am I?" little Alice said to herself as she slowly woke up; and instead of a street and chimney pots there were the fields and the big sun peeping in at her. And when she got up, there would be the farm, with the horses and the cows. It is lovely to wake up on the first day of a holiday.

"'Where am I?' little Alice said to herself."

LAZY DAYS IN THE SUMMER

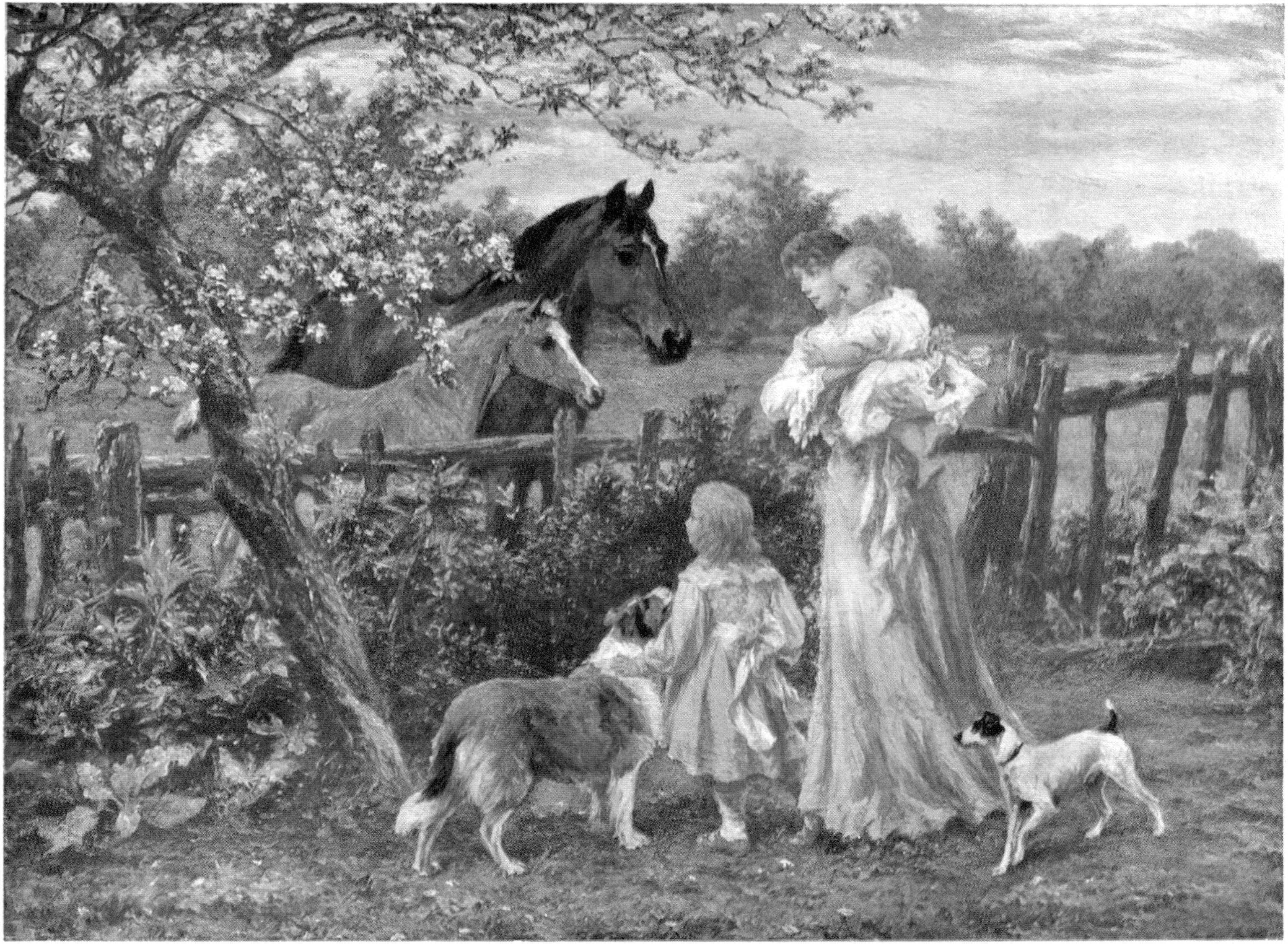

EARLY MORNING WITH THE ANIMALS

POPPIES IN THE WHEAT FIELD

AN AFTERNOON STORY

When Granny was a Little Girl...

WHEN Granny was a little girl,
　　She did just as she should.
I really think she must have been
　　Most 'ceptionally good.

She never lost her temper
　　And she never tore her frocks,
She loved to do plain sewing
　　And she always darned her socks.

She never went for walks unless
    Her hands were neatly gloved,
Rice pudding was her fav'rite dish,
    And prunes she simply *loved!*

She never used a slangy word
    'Cept—sometimes—" Fiddlesticks ! "
She went to bed at seven o'clock
    And rose again at six.

When Granny tells me all these things
  She shakes her head at me,
And says " Alas ! You're not at all
  The child *I* used to be ! "

       *   *   *   *   *

But *I* feel sure she quite forgets
  Her *naughty* deeds, you know,
For Granny was a little girl
  Just sixty years ago !

" SHE LOVED TO DO PLAIN SEWING."

BUNNIKIN

 Bunnikin was a little white rabbit. He was made of plush, and he belonged to Baby Bunting.

One day, when Baby Bunting had been playing in the garden, Bunnikin was left out there, all alone. The other toys had been cleared away and taken indoors, but Bunnikin was forgotten and there he lay, beneath a bush, with only his little white ears showing.

By and by it began to get dark, and as Bunnikin lay there he could see a brown rabbit—a real live wild one—squeezing himself through a little hole in the fence.

Bunnikin gave a little cough.

The brown rabbit nearly jumped out of his skin.

Then he caught sight of Bunnikin's white ears, and came towards him.

"How you startled me!" he said.

"I'm sorry," said Bunnikin, "but I did want to speak to you. I've never spoken to a **real** rabbit before. You see, I'm——" he lowered his voice—— **"I'm** only made of plush, and my inside is just sawdust, I'm afraid, so I can't run about and have jolly times like you do. I wish I could."

"Poor little thing," said the brown rabbit, pityingly. "Would you like to come back with me to my burrow? I think p'rhaps we could find room for you, though our family **is** rather a large one."

"Indeed I would!" said Bunnikin. "I'd love to live with you, to be a real rabbit!"

So the brown rabbit dragged little Bunnikin through the hole in the fence away to his burrow, and introduced him to his wife. She didn't seem very pleased.

"My **dear** Whiskers" she said, to her husband, "what will you do next? We've got eight children as it is, and no spare bed. He'll have to sleep with them, I suppose," and she pulled Bunnikin along a dark stuffy passage and into a tiny underground room where there were already eight little rabbits tucked up in bed, peeping over the blankets at him with bright, wide-awake eyes. Mrs. Rabbit drew back the sheet and popped Bunnikin in among the others, and then she went off to her supper. And oh! **how** those little rabbits teased poor Bunnikin! When

She
didn't
seem
very
pleased.

they found he could not walk, because he was only made of plush and saw-dust, they just bit him and tickled him and pommelled him and teased him until the tears poured down his little cheeks, and he longed, oh, **so** much, to be back at home once more. Finally, when they got sleepy, they just kicked him out of bed, and he lay on the earthy floor and longed for the morning.

And when the brown rabbit came in to waken his children, Bunnikin said in a wee quivery voice, "Oh, do **please** take me home."

So the brown rabbit dragged Bunnikin back to the garden again, and there Baby Bunting found him when he came out to play.

But Bunnikin never told Baby Bunting about his strange adventure.

DANDY

Now Dandy can do twice as much
    As other horses do,
For other horses carry one
    But Dandy carries two.

Then I'm in front as driver
    And sister rides behind,
And off we go together
    And Dandy doesn't mind.

If we shall go
    to India,
Or Africa or
    Spain,
He takes us
    there to-
    gether
And brings us
    back again.

THE MARCH OF THE MINCE-PIES

It was, perhaps, because Janet had been helping Mother to cook for Christmas. Suddenly she saw strange soldiers marching past her while the

"Funniest Sight of all, Mince-pies carrying Forks on their Shoulders."

band played a long march tune. The soldiers were plum-puddings, sausage-rolls, and, funniest sight of all, mince-pies carrying forks on their shoulders. They smiled at Janet and said: "Can you tell us the way to Janet's house?"

"I am Janet," she said, or thought she was saying, when suddenly, the voices of the mince-pies became the voice of Nurse saying: "Christmas Eve! up you get!"

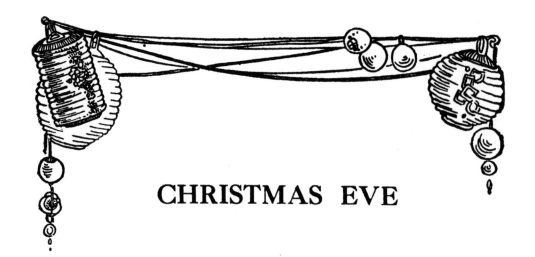

CHRISTMAS EVE

OH! Christmas Eve is the night of nights,
  Up on the hill o' dreams,
And a waiting world, with stockings and socks,
  Climbs up in the cold moonbeams:

Climbs up to the little brown house at the top
  And bangs away at its doors,
And with laugh and a shout, those stockings to fill,
  Call out old Santa Claus.

WHEN ROBIN SINGS

When in the morning light you hear
Cock-robin singing loud and clear,
And look into the garden dim
You'll see two fairies near to him:
With pearly wings with sweet-blue
   stripes,
Wee Tinkle-tinkle plays the pipes,
And singing on the bough as well,
You'll see the fairy Claribel;
And all the three sing sweet and strong
And all the garden rings with song.

FEEDING THE ROBINS

LITTLE MISS MOLLY

NAUGHTY MOLLY.

MOST folks think
some beastie
Isn't very nice.
Molly hated spiders,
Nurse detested mice.

One day little Molly
Caught a poor wee mouse,
Hiding in a flower-pot
Just outside the house.

"I'm so glad I've found you,"
Naughty Molly said.
"Now I'm going to put you
Into Nurse's bed!"

Back she pulled the bed-clothes,
Mousie gave a squeak,

Molly dropped him quickly
  With a frightened shriek!—
For a great big spider
  Ran out on the bed,
From beneath the blanket—
  Molly quickly fled!

  .   .   .   .   .

"Wonder why you gave her
  Such a dreadful fright?"
Said the mouse. "I think, though,
  That it serves her right!"
"Hurry!" said the spider.
  "We had better go,
Though I can't imagine
  Why they hate us so!"

THE TRAIN IN THE NURSERY

When Derry and his sister Marian came back from the seaside, they were rather dumpy at first. Even the railway journey had been exciting.

"S'pose we play at trains," Marian said.

And Derry said "S'pose we do!"

"Here is the trunk, Derry," his sister said, "and you must sit on it, while I get the train started." The nursery made the station; Derry sat on the box and Marian got everything ready.

"Now you must stop being a passenger, Derry," she said, "and be the guard."

Derry knew exactly what to do; he seized his bell and waved the flag, and the train, with all its passengers and all the luggage began to move.

"Derry waved the flag."

They took a very short time to reach the seaside. But when the train stopped, Marian got out with her bag and umbrella, and they played at being by the sea with donkeys to ride and castles to build.

And although it was only make-believe, they both thoroughly enjoyed the game and felt ever so much more cheerful by the time Nurse came in to put them to bed.

"Marian got out with her bag and umbrella."

THE BUS

Bobby with his cart one day
Met some elves upon his way
" If you want a lift," he cried,
" There is room for three inside."

FROM OVER THE SEAS

One day there was a birthday in our house, and we said that we and our friends would all dress up and be like children in other countries. Dressing up is always good fun; and the older people, mummies and daddies and aunties, all helped. When the day came, it was just as if we had all come from over the seas.

We pretended that we were all strangers, but sometimes the very tiny ones forgot; and little Enid, whispered: "Who'm I? And where do I come from?"

And her sister told her: "You are a Swede and you come from Swede-land." But her brother, who knows almost everything, said it was not Swede-land but Sweden.

We were very good friends all the same; and when we asked daddy how we should play at being children from other lands, he said that we ought to be just as we always are, because, he says, boys and girls everywhere are very much the same.

Old Mother Hubbard

Old Mother Hubbard
Went to the cupboard
To get her poor doggie a bone.
But when she got there
The cupboard was bare,
And so the poor doggie had none.

She went to the baker's
To buy him some bread,
But when she
came back
The poor
dog was dead.

She went to the joiner's,
To buy him a coffin.
But when
she came back
The poor dog was laughing.

She took a clean dish
To get him some tripe.
But when she came back
He was smoking a pipe.

She went to the tavern
For white wine and red
But when she came back
The dog stood on his head.

120

She went to the barber's
To buy him a wig
But when she came back
He was dancing a jig.

She went to the cobbler's
To buy him some shoes,
But when she came back
He was reading the news.

She went to the hatter's
To buy him a hat,
But when she came back
He was feeding the cat.

She went to
the fruiterer's
To buy him some
fruit
But when she came back
He was playing the flute.

She went to the fishmonger's,
To buy him some
fish,
But when she
came back
He was licking the dish.

The dame made a curtsey
The dog made a bow.
The dame said "your servant!"
The dog said " Bow-wow!

"'I am an Elf', said the little creature."

NEW STORIES FOR THE ELVES

"I am an Elf," said the little creature, "and I live in a mushroom; now who are you?"

"I am Harry," the boy answered, "and I am not so little as you——"

"I am big for an Elf," the little thing replied, "but won't you tell me a tale. I know all the tales of the elves."

So Harry told the Elf all the tales he knew, till suddenly he looked, and there was only the mushroom and little Alice, who had crept up to listen, too, for the Elf was flying away on his dragonfly.

"The Elf was flying away on his dragonfly."

LULLABY

Hush-a-bye, Baby,
  Shut sleepy eyes,
Wee stars are twinkling
  Up in the skies.

Roses are nodding
  Their drowsy heads,
Birds, too, are sleeping
  Tucked in their beds.

King-cups are folding
Petals of gold
Small woolly lambkins
Sleep in the fold.

Hush-a-bye Baby,
Shut sleepy eyes,
Little stars watch you
Up in the skies—

"Hush, little Baby,"
They seem to say,
"Night-time's for sleeping,
Day-time for play!"

Hush, then, my Baby . . . .

. . . . .

There, that is right.
Sweetly he's sleeping . . .
Baby, Good-night.

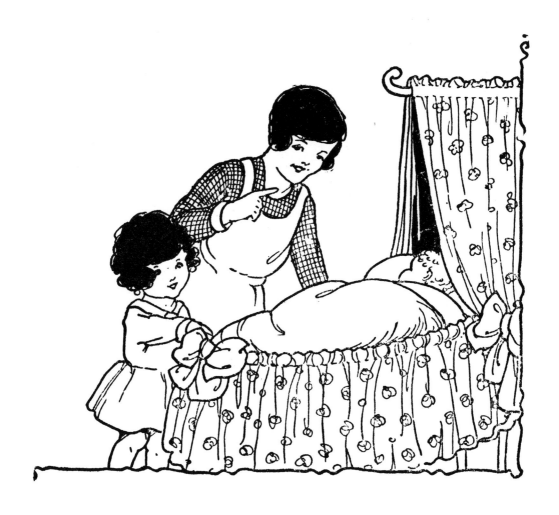

WAITING

Alice was alone, but she would not leave her hassock. Her daddy had been playing with her, when someone came in a hurry to fetch him, for her daddy was a doctor.

"Stop here till I come back," he said. Alice knew he could not have forgotten her, but she was very glad when he returned, he had been a long way, he said; and she was very proud when he added that she had been good to wait so bravely. Waiting is, certainly, not much fun and most children just hate it, but if your daddy were a doctor, too, you'd soon learn to wait patiently like little Alice.

"Alice would not leave her hassock."

ALICE PLAYS WHILE SHE WAITS

ADVENTURES IN THE PLAY ROOM

DAPPLE'S ADVENTURE.

DAPPLE, the wooden horse, had made up his mind to have an adventure. It was a jolly day—warm and sunny—and his little master, Jerry, had gone for a pic-nic. All was quiet in the nursery, so now was Dapple's chance.

"I'll cross the common first," he said to himself, "and have a word with the geese by the pond. They'll be very pleased to see me, I expect."

But when Dapple reached the pond, the geese hissed loudly, and the old gander pecked his leg.

"What are you doing here?" he asked.

"I've come to visit you," said Dapple. "It's a nice afternoon, and I thought I'd have a breath of fresh air."

All the geese cackled with laughter.

"Ho-ho!" they cried. "Fancy a silly wooden toy like you coming to call on us! Go home to your nursery!"

"I can see some of my relations coming," Dapple said huffily—and he went to meet Bess, the grey mare, and Snowball, her foal.

"Oh, mother, do look!" said Snowball, as Dapple drew near. "What a queer little creature! What is he?"

The grey mare stopped and stared at the wooden horse, who was beginning to wish he had never come out.

"Who are you?" she asked.

Dapple's wooden legs suddenly felt very shaky. "I–I'm—"

"He's a relation of yours, he says," cackled the geese, enjoying the joke.

But Bess did not look as if she thought it a joke at all.

"Impudence!" she said. And she waded into the pond and began to drink.

But Snowball turned her back on the wooden horse and gave a playful kick—and—up, up, up went Dapple, into the air, and then—splash—he had fallen into the water.

The geese cackled more than ever now, and Dapple dragged himself out of the pond feeling very sorry for himself indeed. One of his wooden legs had been broken in the fall and his tail had come unstuck and was now lying at the bottom of the pond.

Ten minutes later a very woe-be-gone and draggled Dapple crept into the nursery once more.

"What has happened?" asked Teddy.

But Dapple would not speak.

The other toys brought some dust- ers from the dolls' house and dried him as best they could, and when Jerry came back the little wooden horse was standing in his corner just as he had left him.

But Jerry could never find out how Dapple had broken his leg, nor how he had lost his tail.

THE BROWNIES LEARN TO COOK

The Brownies had a great treat one year. When summer came, a friend of theirs said: "Brownies, I am going away and you can live in my house; you can play in the garden and gather the fruit, but you

"Two of them said to the others one day: 'All of you run away and play.'"

must do all your work yourselves, cooking and all that."

The Brownies were ever so excited when the time came. They simply loved their house, but at first they were not so clever at cooking.

But two of them said to the others one day: "All of you run away and play, and come back when the clock strikes twelve."

And when the clock struck twelve, the Brownies came in hungry and found the two Cooks with crisp brown rolls, big and round. And each of them had a roll for himself and, when they had eaten them, they said: "Three cheers for the two Cooks!"

Then the two successful Cooks taught the others how to bake and fry, but they never told them how they themselves had learnt the art of cooking.

"Each of them had a roll for himself."

TWO TEDDIES

WOIREDEDDIESRYINGOROOAUNON.

When you have put a certain letter in the above sentence ten times over, it will read quite sensibly

SAMMY'S IDEA

When little Sam on Christmas Eve
    Went off upstairs to bed
He thought he'd made a lovely plan,
    And this is what he said,

" I'll hang up both my socks, of course,
    But that won't be enough,
For Santa Claus is sure to bring
    Me lots and lots of stuff?—

—And so I'll find some stockings, too,
   And hang them by my bed,
A pair of Daddy's on each side
   And one above my head,

And then, in case *that* isn't quite
   Enough for him to fill,
I'll put out both my Wellingtons,
   And those of brother Bill.—

And then what lots of things I'll find
   On Christmas Day," he said,—

Those socks and
boots and stock-
ings all
Quite full be-
side my
bed!"

*   *   *   *   *

Quite early, then, on Christmas-day
Young Sammy woke, and said,
"I *wonder* what I'll find inside
The things all round my bed,

There will be crowds and crowds of toys
—Yes, there are sure to be!—
I'll turn the light on, then, hooray,
I'll see what I shall see!"

*   *   *   *   *

BUSY LITTLE SISTERS

Here are Betty and Beatrice Barr,
A hard-working couple they are !
They make tea-cloths and cosies,
Embroidered with roses,
For many a Sale or Bazaar.

BABY

When in the garden baby lies,
And looks right up into the skies,
She stretches out her arms and legs,
And for all lovely things she begs.
For waving leaves and clouds so high;
For birds that sail across the sky.
And when she cannot catch these
                      things,
Then sister to her gently brings
A flower for baby's hands to keep
Till baby tired shall fall asleep.

A SUNNY CORNER

PLAYTIME FOR PUSSY

PUSSY AND THE GOBLIN

When Pussy goes out for a walk,
    I wonder whom our Pussy sees,
With whom does little Pussy talk
    When leaves fall from the trees
    And winds are blowing free?

I think the goblins when they play,
    Must tease our little Pussy-cat
In the stormy Autumn day
    When the leaves fall pitter-pat
    Dancing round her just like that!

THE STORY OF GILBERT GOSLING

Gilbert Gosling was on his way home from school.

It was such a lovely day that he went the long way round, past Reynard's Hollow.

"Good morning, little Gosling," said a voice.

 Gilbert did not know that the fox was an enemy. He went indoors with him to have some lemonade.

"Now I've got you," said Reynard, and he tied Gilbert up to the wood pile outside the back door.

 Then he went off to fetch his biggest saucepan, and some herbs, and some apples for apple sauce.

Poor Gilbert Gosling shed big tears.

"Can I help you?" asked a voice.

It was Fanny Field-Mouse. With her sharp teeth she bit right through the cord that held Gilbert prisoner.

Then they raced off together across the field.

Mrs. Goose gave Fanny a whole wheel-barrow full of corn, she was so pleased with her.

And Fanny trundled it home.

But Reynard was so angry that he kicked the saucepan right over the top of the house.

And up into a fir tree.

And there it is, to this day. Mr. and Mrs. Squirrel found it, and use it to keep their nuts in.

PEEP-BO!

Before our Baby, who is very, very small, has her bath, Mummy lets us come and see her and play with her on the rug before the fire, but not for long.

What we like to do best of all is to get a big hat which has always been one of our play-things in the nursery, the biggest hat that was ever seen.

And we put it over baby, till she creeps out and we clap our hands and say:

" Peep-bo ! "

THE WISE LITTLE MOUSE

Said Mr. Thomas Pussy-Cat
  To little Mr. Mouse:
"Pray, won't you come
          inside and see
My nicely furnished
          house?
The place is most
          attractive,
  And my neighbours
          you will be.
For now, you know, I've
          come to **live**
  In this locality."

Said Mr. Mouse: "I'm sorry, Sir,
  But I must really hurry,
I've left my little wife alone,
  And she's inclined to worry.

So shall I come another
day?"
Said Pussy: "Yes,
pray **do**!
I'm glad we shall be
neighbours,
For I like the look of you."

But Mr. Mouse went running home
To tell his wife the news.
"We'll have to move at once," he said,
"There is no time to lose.
So get the children ready, dear,
As quickly as you can,
And I will shift the
furniture
And pack it in the
van."

"I'd like to see that
        mouse again,"
Said Puss, "I'll
        find his house.
I've had no meat at
        all to-day,
I'd **like** a joint of mouse!"

.   .   .   .   .

But Mr. Thomas
        Pussy-Cat
That meal will
        never get!
For when he reached
        the little house,
He found it was "TO LET."

THE SEE-SAW

All that you need is a plank of wood
On a piece of a big tree-stump,
And you go up and down, down and
up, as you should
Or perhaps you come down with a
bump:
While you sing all the time
This beautiful rhyme:

Me and you, you and me
See-saw, saw-see.

BABY BUNNIES AT HOME

Mother Bunny makes a very comfy little nursery for her babies by scraping out a soft earthy burrow. This she lines with some of her own fur, to keep her children warm— for at first the babies are quite bare— they have no fur of their own at all!

By-and-bye, when the little ones' coats have grown, Mother Bunny takes

them out with her to nibble the short sweet grass. How they love to tumble and play about! They have such games together, and Mummy watches them as they play, and looks very proud of them indeed.

But if a stranger is seen anywhere about, Mother Bunny tells her children that danger is near, and in less time that it takes to write it all the little bob-bity tails have disappeared down the bur-row again!

POOR PERCY

Poor Percy
Pythagoras Payne,
I fear he could not
have been sane!
He bought a balloon
And set off for the Moon,
But has never been heard
of again.

CHASING HIS BALLOON

NIGHT TIME WITH THE FAIRIES

THE MAGIC LOOKING-GLASS

Marigold was the prettiest of all the little Flower Fairies who waited on the Fairy Queen—and she knew it, too. It was such a pity, for she grew more and more conceited, and was always peeping at 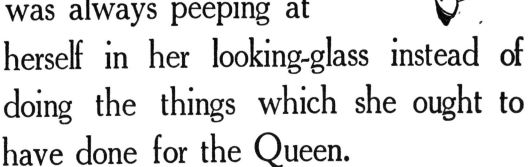 herself in her looking-glass instead of doing the things which she ought to have done for the Queen.

One day an inquisitive little elf happened to pass her window just as

Marigold was trying on a new frock in front of her looking-glass.

"She ought to be helping the other Flower Fairies," said the elf to himself. "They are busy weaving a gossamer gown for the Queen," and off he flew and told the Queen what Marigold was doing.

The Fairy Queen was quite angry.

"She is getting **much** too vain," she said. "I must put a stop to it."

So that very night, when Marigold was fast asleep in bed, the Queen sent a trusty gnome who flew in through Marigold's window and then magicked her looking-glass.

The next morning, when the little Flower Fairy awoke, she went straight to her glass as usual, expecting to find

What a dreadful shock she had!

 that she was more beautiful than ever. But oh, what a dreadful shock she had! The face that looked back at her was old and ugly, with a long hooked nose, and the hair, instead of being a mass of golden curls, hung about her face in a few straggling black wisps.

"Oh dear, oh dear," sobbed Marigold. "Somebody has cast a spell over me! Whatever **shall** I do?" For she did not know that it was only the looking-glass that had been magicked—

she herself was just as pretty as ever.

She dressed in a hurry and went off to Court. The  Queen had told the other Flower Fairies what she had done, so they all pretended that Marigold was looking quite different, and told her how sorry they were that she had lost her good looks.

"Never mind," said the Fairy Queen quite kindly. "Handsome is as handsome does, you know, and perhaps, now that you are no longer beautiful, you will think about

 your duty more."

Marigold hung her head and blushed with shame.

. . . . .

But it did her a lot of good. She could not bear to look in her looking-glass now, and she soon grew to be the most hardworking, painstaking, kind little Flower Fairy at Court.

Then the Queen sent the gnome to unmagic the looking-glass, and once more Marigold saw herself as she really was.

But it didn't make any difference. She had learnt her lesson, and she is still the sweetest of all the Flower Fairies.

THE BROWNIE PIPER.

I'M a merry little fellow,
  Leader of the Brownie band,
Dressed in green and primrose yellow,
  With a pipe in either hand.

When the children all are sleeping,
  Dreaming sweetly through the night.
And the big round moon is keeping
  Field and wood aflood with light.

Wondrous music, airs entrancing,
  On my magic pipes I play;
And I set the Brownies dancing
  Gaily till the dawn of day.

Round a mushroom tripping lightly,
  Hand in hand they love to go;
To my strains so blithe and sprightly
  Keeping time on pointed toe.

Faster still and faster ever,
  Whilst the stars send down their rays,
For the Brownies tire never
  When the Brownie Piper plays!

When our joyous dance is over,
  Oft we have a game or two;
Playing leapfrog o'er the clover,
  Or at ball with drops of dew.

Till, the glad new day proclaiming,
  All the cocks begin to crow;
Then, when eastern skies are flaming,
  Back to Brownie-land we go.

Do you want to hear me playing,
  Or to see the Brownies dance?
Well, perhaps (there is no saying),
  You may some day get the chance!

FUN ON THE ICE.

IT'S really very nice
  To picnic on the ice,
If you're clad in cosy fur from head to toes,
  Just like the polar bear,
  In his coat of shaggy hair,
Of course *he* doesn't worry if it snows!
  And you'd love the Arctic weather
  If you'd got a gown of feather
Like these penguins so respectable and neat.
  On the frozen floes you'd trot
  And often get quite hot
And never be afraid of chilblained feet.
  Or, if you were a seal,
  The frost you'd never feel,
For your sealskin suit would fit without a fold.
  In the ice-holes you could dive,
  Catching fishes all alive,
And never stand a chance of catching cold.
  Now, dancing's quite the rage—
  Observe the picture page—
With bears and seals and penguins at the Pole,
  And when Christmas comes along
  Each obliges with a song,
And it's quite a good performance on the whole.

FUN·ON·THE·ICE

177

THE THIRSTY FAIRY

I had a picnic in a
field
Alone, the other
day
(Excepting for my
dolly, who
Is named Chris-
tina May).

I took my sewing
with me there.
(A little frock of
blue
I'm making for Christina May,
With hat to match it, too.)

And down we sat upon the grass,
My dolly dear, and I,
With nothing near us 'cept the birds,
And one blue butterfly.

For tea there was a mug of milk,
 A scone and currant bun,
"To have a picnic all alone,"
 I thought, "Is rather fun."

Then, suddenly, I saw that I
 Was not alone at all!—
A tiny fairy stood quite near,
 Upon a ruined wall.

And looked at us with wond'ring
 eyes. . . .
 I said "Oh fairy, dear,
Do come and talk to us. You need
 Not have a scrap of
 fear.

I should so love to
 talk to you,
 And touch you if
 you're real,

And p'rhaps, dear fairy. You would
    like
To share our little meal?"

She fluttered down (her wings were
    gold,
Her hair like yellow silk),
And stood upon the handle of
My little mug of milk.

And then she stooped, and tried to reach
The milk so creamy white.
I was afraid she'd tumble in—
It gave me such a fright.

Then, in a little
　　silv'ry voice
She said "Oh,
　　would you mind
My having just a
　　drop of milk?—
I'm sure that you
　　are kind—"

But, poor wee thing,
　　although she tried,
She could not reach
　　to drink,
And how to help her
　　I could not
For just one moment
　　think.

And then I knew!
　　I lifted her
And sat her on my
　　knee,
Then drew the silver
　　thimble off
That Mummy gave
　　to me—

And dipped it in the
mug of milk
And filled it in a
trice . . . .
And *how* that fairy
drank it down!
—"It *is* so cool and
nice!"

She said, "and I was
overcome
With thirst, this
sunny day.
I'm sure I thank you *very* much!"
And then she flew away.

* * * *

We've been to look for
her, since then,
Well, almost ev'ry
day.
But I have never seen
her—Nor
Has dear Christina
May.

A PICNIC IN THE GARDEN

THE LAVENDER BUSH GIRLS

THE LAND OF DREAMS

DAY-DREAMING BY THE RIVER

IF ONLY!

WERE I not so big—but only
    Say just one foot, or so—
Oh, the lovely nooks I'd visit,
    And the homes to which I'd go!

    I'd enter bunnies' burrows,
        Oh, just wouldn't it be fun?
    And I'd cuddle all their babies,
        And tame them every one.

    I'd find a hollow tree-trunk
        If I hunted all the day,
    And climb the mossy staircase
        Where the little squirrels play.

They would take me to their larder,
  Give me nuts and fruit to eat—
What a much more tasty dinner
  Than potatoes, greens and meat!

Then I'd find a pool all shady,
  And perhaps a frog would rise
With a coat all green and shiny,
  And unwinking goggle eyes;

Perhaps he would invite me
  To his home among the slime;
I don't think I'd accept—no,
  I would say I hadn't time!

I would romp among the daisies
  With the little harvest-mice,
And the moles and little lizards
  And—oh, everything that's nice,

But just merely talking of it,
  And just longing will not do.
I must go and find a fairy
  Who will make my wish
          come true!

OFF TO THE HAY FIELD.

MY BABY

When Baby was in bed last night,
    He thought he'd have some fun.
(I saw the room at eight o'clock,
    I'll tell you what he'd done :)

He'd scrambled from his little cot,
    Right on to Mummy's bed,
And there he found a counterpane
    Of dark blue silk was spread.

He rumpled it, and all the sheets,
   And piled them in a mound,
Then switched on the electric light,
   And slid down to the ground.

And then he made a bundle of
   His Mummy's coat and hat,
And rolled them underneath the bed
   (The hat was squashed quite flat).

But Baby did not feel at all
　Ashamed of what he'd done.
To make a ball of Mummy's clothes
　Was really rather fun.

A parcel, too, which lay just near,
　He opened, and with glee,
He spread it out upon the floor,
　For everyone to see.

The basket of waste paper, next,
　He emptied on the ground.
Then, turning, such a *lovely* thing,
　To play with, Baby found!

What else is there
that I can do?
This *is* a jolly
game!"
And then he turned
his head . . . .
Into
The room, his
Mummy came.

She looked at him.   He looked at her,
And then he gravely said,
"O-ooh *Ba-by!*"   Just like that—and
shook
His curly little head,—

And looked as solemn as a Judge
And just as though he thought
That someone else had done the things,
And not that *he'd* been caught!

APSE

NABSE

SHER DISA

PINS RUT

CESTULET

Old Mr Bunny is taking some goodies home to his family. If you want to know what he has got in his barrow, you must put the jumbled letters in their right order.

CONNIE THE COOK

If you put the above five lots of letters in the right order, you will see five of the ingredients in Connie's cake.

CARLO AND THE KITTENS

I AM known on both sides of the street—
" That's Carlo. Oh ! isn't he sweet ? "
    I often hear said
    (As I'm carried or led)
By those whom I happen to meet.

I'm of high if not royal descent,
And when to a Dog-Show I went,
    I took a first prize,
    Which, I will not disguise,
To do was my aim and intent.

The greatest attention I'm shown ;
I've a comb and a brush of my own ;
    I have chicken and milk
    And a cushion of silk
Which is kept for my service alone.

CARLO AND THE KITTENS.

The two kittens, Flossy and Fluff,
Can hardly admire me enough ;
    They gambol and play
    At my feet and display
Delight if I only say " Wuff !

Though the cat is a creature I find
As a rule not at all to my mind,
    To kittens like these,
    Who endeavour to please,
I am, all admit, very kind.

Miss
Winifred
Willoughby
Wright,
Made a
cake so
remarkably
light,—
That it
rose
through
the
air,
And to her
despair,
Drifted
right away
out of
her sight!

PANICKY

POPPY!

Miss Poppy Penelope Price,
Is dreadfully frightened of mice.
If she hears a faint squeak
She's too trembly to speak,
But gets up on a chair in a trice!

H.G.C.
Marsh
Lambert

199

SOME FOUR-FOOTED BABIES.

This lively little pup will
be a great big hound
one day.

The fluffy kitten to a cat
will grow, too,
Sad to say.

It's hard to think the
frisky lamb
Will be a sheep sedate.

To tell you that this
baby pig
Will be a sow—I hate!

The pretty little leveret
Will grow to be a
hare.

This woolly
cub, if all
goes well,

Quite soon will be a bear.

The colt in just a few
months' time
Will find he is a horse.

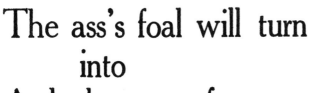

The ass's foal will turn
into
A donkey too, of course.

The little fawn will
grow to be
A great big antlered
deer.

The calf, before so very
long,
Will be a cow, I fear.

And oh ! It makes me
feel quite sad,
Whatever shall I do ?
In just a few years' time,
I s'pose,
I shall be grown up
too !

A RIDE ACROSS THE FIELDS

HELPING GRANNY

BABY-BOY AND THE BUNNIES.

"I'D love to find some primroses,"
Said Nell. "I b'lieve we could
A little farther on you know,
Inside this shady wood."
Said Nancy: "Baby's fast asleep.
We'll leave him.
He'll be good."

The little sisters
went away.
And Baby-Boy
awoke
To see a bunny
rabbit there

A-peeping round
an oak.
He gave a little
squeal of joy,
It really was a
joke!

Then off the little bunny hopped
    As fast as he could go,
And called his friends and neighbours out
    And said, "Do come—for oh !–
There is the dearest Baby here,
    And all alone, d'you know !"

So lots of other rabbits came
    And peeped around the tree,

And Baby clapped his little hands
And shrieked aloud with glee.
"Just hark! There's Baby-Boy," cried
Nell,
"What can the matter be?"

They both came back to Baby-Boy
To see a funny sight—
A host of rabbits, big and small,
Were sitting round
the mite!
But when the bunnies
saw them, they
Skipped off in
sudden fright!

FLOWERS AND FAIRIES

Under a very big mushroom lay
Little boy Tom on a summer day;

Spending one or two lazy hours
Pulling to pieces lovely flowers;

Till a tiny fairy said to him: " Please
Don't tear to pieces the flowers like
these.

"Flowers are the houses of fairies like
me,
And without them where should we
fairies be?"

C. S. Rhodes

THE FLOWER FAIRIES

JANE was working in her garden, when, suddenly, she saw something very strange. In the garden border was a big snail, and on the snail sat a tiny fairy. Behind the snail, pushing it along, was another fairy. And they were both trying to make the snail move faster.

"Hurry! Hurry! Hurry!" said the fairy on the snail's back. "Or we shall

"'HURRY! HURRY! HURRY!' SAID THE
FAIRY ON THE SNAIL'S BACK."

never get there in time." And Jane thought that they certainly wouldn't, for the snail was going so slowly.

"Why don't you fly?" said Jane. "You've both got wings. You'd get there much quicker without the snail."

"Yes, but it is the snail that is important," said the fairies. "Little Princess Fair-As-The-Day has been caught by a wicked witch. The witch has put her in the middle of a toadstool ring and enchanted the toadstools so that she cannot move out of it. When the sun sets to-night, she is going to turn her into a bramble bush. The fairies are terribly unhappy about it. The witch has made an enchantment that fairies can't break. We're trying to find some kind of creature that will eat the toadstools. But none of the creatures we've found so far will touch them because they are a poisonous kind of toad-stool. Snails can eat most things without hurting themselves. So we are all of us flying every-where to try and find snails. But if all the snails are as slow as this one, I'm afraid we'll never get there in time."

Jane had a splendid idea.

"Have you tried salt on the toadstools?" she said. "Daddy sprinkles salt over the weeds on the pathway sometimes to make them die."

"Oh, could

"AWAY THEY FLEW TO THE HILL WHERE THE PRINCESS WAS IMPRISONED."

you give us some to try on the toadstools ? "
said the fairies. And Jane ran and got a
packet of salt, while the fairies fetched all
the other fairies to come and help. Jane
poured the salt into the fairies' hands, and
away they flew to the hill where the poor
little Princess was imprisoned.

After the fairies had gone, Jane went on
working in the garden. When the sun began
to go down, she heard a rush of wings above
her head, and looking up, she saw a fairy on
the back of a dragonfly. After him came
lots of other fairies with smiling, happy
faces.

"JANE SAW A FAIRY ON THE BACK OF A
DRAGONFLY."

"It's all right!" they cried. "The salt worked beautifully.

As soon as we sprinkled it on the toadstools, the spell broke, and the little Princess was free. We've taken her back to her father

"AFTER HIM CAME LOTS OF FAIRIES."

and mother and now we've come to tell you. We're all *so* grateful to you! And as a reward for your cleverness we're going to bring you a nice dream every night for the rest of your life."

And they did—and do still. And if you ever come across Jane, you'll know why it is that she never minds going to bed. It is because she always has such lovely dreams at night.

BRUNO HAS A BUMP

They were very unkind to old Bruno
one day,
When he sat on a chair in the course
of their play
And they crept up behind him and
pulled it away,
And Bruno sat bump on the ground.

When they saw what they'd done, they
came back with a rush
And they lifted him up and they gave
him a brush,

And said they
were sorry
and also said,
"Hush!"
When they
lifted him up
from the
ground.

THE HOME OF THE FISHES

When you go
out in
dreams,
You may go
near
or far;
To the ends
of the
earth
Or away to a star.

But you ought not to go
Away under the sea
For the fishes dislike
To see you and me.

"Now what are you doing
Down here?" they will say;
And we shall be frightened
And swim right away.

"'HAVE YOU HEARD THE NEWS?' THEY SAID."

PEGGY'S PUPPY

"HAVE you heard the news?" said the white dog from the first house in the street to the black retriever. "Peggy-at-the-other-end-of-the-Road has lost her puppy."

"That's bad! Where has she lost him?" asked the black retriever, who lived at Number Two.

"Nobody knows," said the white dog. "Nobody has seen him since breakfast time, and Peggy-at-the-other-end-of-the-Road is crying her eyes out."

" Dear, dear ! " said the retriever. " Let's go and tell the pug at Number Three, and see if he knows anything about him."

So the white dog and the black retriever went to see the pug at Number Three.

" Have you heard the news ? " they said. " Peggy-at-the-other-end-of-the-Road has lost her puppy, and no-body seems to know where he has gone to.

" Dear, dear ! That's bad ! " said the pug. " Let's go and tell the dog at Number Four, and see if he can tell us anything about him."

So the three dogs went to see the dog at Number Four. But the dog at Number Four didn't know anything about Peggy's puppy, nor did the dog at Number Five, nor the dog at Number Six. None of the dogs in the road had seen him that morning, though they all turned out and went along with the white dog and the pug and the retriever to seek him.

"We'll go and see if we can find him," said the dogs. And they all ran off, all of them together. And sure enough, just round the corner, was Peggy's puppy. He had run after the butcher's boy and a strange dog had rolled him in the gutter, and he was all lost and muddy and miserable. But he was quite safe and sound, and the dogs took him home to Peggy-at-the-other-end-of-the-Road. And Peggy was so pleased to see him. She gave the dogs a biscuit each for having brought him home to her, and then she and her little brother got out the wash-tub and gave the silly little puppy a bath to make him clean again.

"You must *never* run after the butcher's boy

"'YOU MUST NEVER RUN AFTER THE BUTCHER'S BOY AGAIN,' PEGGY TOLD HIM."

again, Peggy told him. And the puppy was so glad to get home again that he never even grumbled at being bathed.

In fact, for some little time afterwards he was so frightened that he would get lost again that he always kept very close to Peggy when she took him out for a walk.

OUT FOR A RUN WITH MY DOG

DOWN ON THE FARM

· TIME · TO · RISE ·

" THE · COCK · DOTH · CROW · TO · LET · YOU · KNOW ·
· IF · YOU · BE · WISE · 'TIS · TIME · TO · RISE. "

A.BOWERLEY

223

MY DREAM CASTLE

I simply love my
castle,
  I think that
you would too,
If only I could show you
  As I'd simply love to do.
But, sad to say, I cannot—
    You'll never meet me
    there—

   .   .   .   .   .   .

Because, you see, my
castle
  Is a castle in the
air!

THE OWL
AND THE MICE

Mr. Wise-Acre, the owl, lived in the ruins of the old church tower and all the day long he would sit and blink sleepily at the sunshine, as a few rays of it found their way into his home. By night, though, he was very wide awake indeed, and woe betide any little stray mouse who ran across his path!

The mice disliked Mr. Wise-Acre very much, and so they used to tease him whenever they could. **That** was only in the day-time, when the owl could scarcely see at all. Then the naughty little mice would come and stand in front of him and say the **rudest** things, knowing quite well that old Wise-Acre couldn't possibly catch them. (He was nearly blind in the day-time, of course).

This went on day after day and the owl got crosser and crosser. But every time he made a furious dash at his little tormentors they only ran away laughing, and so at last he gave it up. But to have to sit quite still and just **endure** it, when the mice were so very rude, was almost more than he could stand.

"You just wait until I catch you!" he would cry angrily, but the mice only laughed again. They knew better than to show themselves to the owl by night, when he could see even better than they could.

But a little fairy who lived in an oak tree near by felt sorry for Mr. Wise-

Acre, and one day she called to see him.

"Excuse my interfering," she said. "But I know someone who could help you. If you will give me a few of your very downiest feathers for a new bed I am making, I will ask my friend to come to your aid."

So Mr. Wise-Acre gave the fairy six lovely downy little feathers, and then she flew off and fetched Thimble-kin, the Elf.

"Who are you?" asked

the owl, blink-
ing at the Elf,
stupidly.

"I'm the
Fairies' spectacle-
maker," answered
Thimblekin, "and I
want you to try on
these glasses." As
he spoke he handed
a pair of big horn-rimmed spectacles to
Mr. Wise-Acre.

The owl put them on. Then he
gave a loud "Tu-whoo" of delight.

"Why—I can see beautifully," he
said—"almost as well as by night!"

"Good!" said Thimblekin and the

 fairy, and they flew off, well pleased with what they had done.

As for the mice, they didn't dare to tease old Wise-Acre any more. It was much too dangerous!

So he went on living quite peacefully in the old church tower, and I daresay he is living there still. In fact, if you should happen to be playing hide and seek there one day (and it's a fine old ruin for hide and seek) you might see Mr. Wise-Acre, yourself! He generally sits on the top stone but one of the old tower, and of course you would know him by the spectacles. I wonder if you ever will?

A SHOWER.

OH, Mrs. Jumbo,
    Can't you run?
A heavy shower
    Has just begun.

Your velvet coat,
    Your frilly skirt,
Will soon be soaked
    With rain and dirt.

Your brollie's such
    A *little* one;
Oh, Mrs. Jumbo—
    Can't you run?

WALKING ON THE TILES

I CAN walk upon the tiles in our hall
  And put a foot on each and miss the
    cracks ;
Or over two at once and never fall,
  Or only walk on reds and not on blacks.

Sometimes I say if I take one step wrong
  A wolf will come and eat me in one bite,
And if I play this game for very long
  It frightens me. *I think he really might.*

My first is in currant, but not in fig,

My second's in sow, but not in pig,

My third is in Goat, but not in ship,

My fourth is in slide, and also in slip

My fifth is in noun, but not in word,

My whole is the name of a dear wee bird.

CAN YOU GUESS THIS LITTLE ACROSTIC?

The answer is: ROBIN

A SCRAPE

Neville ought not to have gone out that morning when nobody was looking in that very muddy lane. He fell down in such a splash. He was muddy all over when he ran back to the house. But nobody had seen him, and that was lucky. So he crept to the bathroom saying to himself: "I will wash it off." So, although he wasn't a bit fond of water, he took the sponge and soap and began to rub himself, and when his mother came in he was almost clean again. And mother didn't even say a word about the dirty towel and the water on the floor.

"Neville took the sponge and began to rub himself."

THE TWO BIRTHDAY PARTIES

ANN was feeling very excited. To-morrow was her birthday, and she was going to have a party. Ever so many boys and girls were coming to tea. Ann had written all the invitation cards herself, and all the children had written back to say that they would be ever so pleased to come.

And now it was half-past three on the afternoon of the day before the party. This time to-morrow the visitors would just be beginning to arrive. Ann was standing in the hall trying to count how many more times the grandfather clock would strike before the party began, when there came a ring at the bell.   There on the door-step was a little boy with a Teddy-bear under one arm, and in a box on wheels which he was dragging behind him, he had a doll.

"Many happy returns of the day, Ann!" he said. "I've brought you two birthday presents. And I wouldn't let Nurse wrap them up, because I thought they'd like to see the house where they're going to live."

And while Ann stood staring at him, two little girls came running up, carrying presents.

"Many happy returns, Ann!" they said. And while they were saying it, up came more children, and more and more, until all the party was there!

"But—but my birthday isn't until to-morrow," said Ann.

"Isn't it? To-day's Wednesday; you said Wednesday on your card," said the children.

And so Ann had. She had made a

"'MANY HAPPY RETURNS OF THE DAY, ANN!' HE SAID."

"NEXT DAY THEY ALL CAME AGAIN."

mistake when she wrote out the cards, and all the children had come on the wrong day.

"Oh dear! And hardly any of the cakes are ready yet. The party will be spoilt!" cried Ann, bursting into tears.

But then Ann's mother came along.

"Never mind! We'll have two parties!" said Ann's mother. "We'll find aprons and overalls for everybody, and you shall all come

into the kitchen and help to make the cakes
and things for Ann's birthday. And to-morrow you shall come again and have the proper
party."

"Oh what fun!" cried the children.
"What a lovely kind of party it will be."
And so it was. And the next day they all
came again and helped to eat the things they
had made. And both parties were so nice
that nobody knew which was the nicer.

And that was how Ann had two parties.

FEEDING SQUIRRELS IN THE PARK

LOOKING AFTER DOLLS AND DOGS

I LIKE TO WASH MY DOLLIES
CLOTHES
AND HANG THEM OUT TO DRY
THEY FLUTTER LIKE WHITE
BUTTERFLIES
AGAINST A PALE BLUE SKY.

AND WHEN THEY'RE DRY
I TAKE THEM IN
AND IRON EACH TUCK & PLEAT
YOU'D KNOW MY DOLLIES
ANYWHERE
SO CLEAN THEY ARE — SO NEAT.

WASHING DAY

"MISS MOLLY McBRIGHT,
    Come out and play."
" I can't," said Miss Molly,
" It's washing day."

                " My dolly's clothes
                Are as black as ink,
                How they get so dirty—
                I cannot think."

" I must scrub and rub
Till they're clean and white,
So leave me alone,"
Said Miss Molly McBright.

SUPPOSING THAT I'D BEEN A BOY

SUPPOSING that I'd been a boy,
   Instead of just a girl, you know,
I'd have no ribbons to annoy,
   I'd have no tiresome curls to blow,
No starchy, prickly pinafores,
No hat or gloves for out-of-doors.

No one would call me " Tomboy Joan ";
   I shouldn't have such things as frocks ;
(If I had boy's clothes of my own

I'd have no need to borrow Jock's !)
I'd stow *such* treasures, old and new,
  In half-a-dozen pockets too !

The boys would let me play with them,
  For girls are never any fun.
And oh ! I needn't learn to hem ! . . .
  A boy may always ride and run,
And leap and climb, like Jock and Mike,
And not be called " unladylike."

"'A funny plant,' said Pussy to himself."

A NARROW ESCAPE

There were three Mice who were playing one day in the green-house, when who should come along but Sooty, the black cat.

"Quick!" called the oldest of the three. "Hide like anything; here, in this flower-pot!"

Before you could squeak, as the mice say, they were buried in the flower-pot. But their long tails were waving in the air, just as if they were growing in the pot.

Pussy passed by with soft steps. "A

funny plant," he said to himself. "Plants don't shake like that; I wonder what it is. Shall I stop to look?"

But Pussy did not stop, because he was in a hurry to get to his tea, or rather his milk. Pit! pat! went his paws in the distance.

Then as soon as he had gone, out popped three tiny heads.

"He's gone," said the first. "Hip hurrah! Lucky for us!" cried the second. "What a silly pussy!" added the third. "But what a narrow escape."

"'But what a narrow escape!' added the third mouse."

THE THREE SCOUTS.

BILL BANTAM, Dicky Duck and Joe
  The Gosling, Scouts all three,
The other afternoon did go
  To see what they could see.

They found a slimy, shiny trail
  Which seemed to wind and wind,
And followed it—and ate the snail,
  And left the shell behind.

And as, delighted with their luck,
  They slowly waddled back
In single file, young Dicky Duck
  Cried, in surprise, " Quack ! Quack !

THE THREE SCOUTS.

" Look at these footprints I have found!
　　Look here, Bill ! Look here, Joe !
An army must have crossed this ground
　　A little while ago.

" Though small in size, it seems to me
　　There must be fifty pairs
At least.　But, though we're only three,
　　For that " said he, " who cares ? "

So, with their eyes upon the ground,
　　Bill, Dick and Joe, with speed,
Set off and—What d'you think they found
　　At last ? A centipede !

THE BROWNIES AND THE BEES

The Busy-body Brownies were walking hand-in-hand,
They saw a funny structure upon a wobbly stand.

" Oh, *dear* ! See here ! " cried all the five, " Whatever
  can it be ? "
Said Brownies Numbers One and Two, " Let's push
  the thing and see."

The Brownies filled the air with noise, the bees with
  angry hum ! ! ! !—
Those Brownies won't be seen again for many days
  to come.

THE GREEN UMBRELLA

"How hot it is," said Maria, the Dutch doll. "I think I'll sit down and rest."

She unfurled her green umbrella as she spoke, and propped it up on the grass behind her head. Then she leant back against a tree and watched the water as the river swirled gently past her. It was singing a soothing little song, and soon Maria fell fast asleep.

She hadn't been asleep more than a minute or two and was having the most

lovely dream when
a mischievous little
Teddy-bear came
along.

"Hurrah! he said
to himself, as he
caught sight of the
green umbrella.
"That's just the thing for me! The
water looks jolly. I'm longing to have a
sail!" and he crept up behind the Dutch
doll and took away the big open umbrella.

He carried it down to the river and
let it float on the top of the water.
Then, just as it left the bank, he hopped
gaily into it and set off on his travels
down the river.

The breeze carried the green umbrella gently along, and Teddy enjoyed

his trip very much at first. But soon a strong wind sprang up, and the umbrella bobbed and jumped on the top of the water, making Teddy feel very ill indeed.

"Oh dear, I don't like this," he said. "I wish I hadn't come!"

But it was no use wishing that. On went the umbrella, on, on, and still the wind rose higher and higher, until Teddy was soaked with the water that splashed over him, and thought every minute that he was going to be drowned.

And then, at last—**Bump!**

The um-brella had grounded against the roots of a willow that grew by the side of the stream, and Teddy rolled stiffly out and prepared to go home. He dragged the green um-brella far up the bank, and was just going to leave it lying in the grass when a voice said: "Here he is!" Looking up, Teddy saw Maria sitting on a wooden horse a few yards away.

She had awakened soon after Teddy had started, and a kind wooden horse which was passing had offered to carry

her along the bank of the river until she should come up with the naughty little Teddy-bear.

"Well, you don't look as if you've enjoyed it," said Maria, severely shaking the water out of her green umbrella as she spoke. "You'd better get home and go to bed, I think!

That was just what Teddy did.

But he caught a dreadful cold all the same, and I don't think he will go for a sail in other people's umbrellas again in a hurry!